Contents

A polar region habitat 4

Polar bear 6

Whale 10

Iceberg 14

Penguin 18

Picture glossary 23

Index 24

A polar region habitat

A polar region is an area of land.
A polar region is very cold.

A polar region has living things.
A polar region has non-living things.

Polar bear

Is a polar bear a living thing?

Does a polar bear need food? *Yes.*
Does a polar bear need water? *Yes.*

Does a polar bear need air? *Yes.*

Does a polar bear grow? *Yes.*

So a polar bear is a living thing.

Whale

humpback whale

Is a whale a living thing?

Does a whale need food? *Yes.*
Does a whale need water? *Yes.*

Does a whale need air? *Yes.*

Does a whale grow? *Yes.*

So a whale is a living thing.

Iceberg

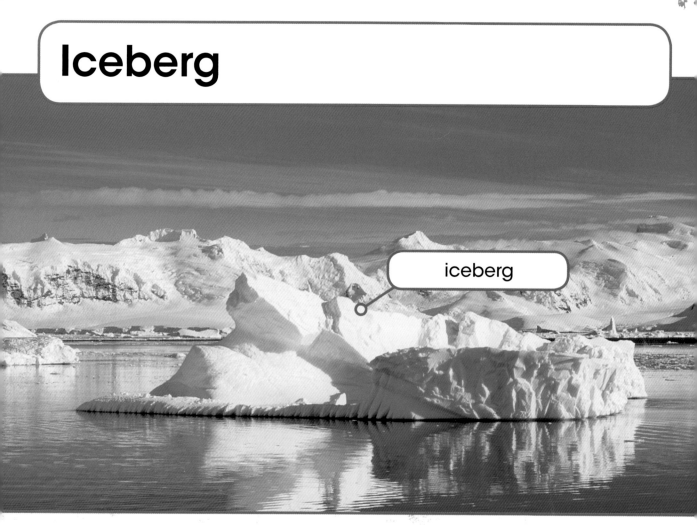

iceberg

Is an iceberg a living thing?

Does an iceberg need food? *No.*
Does an iceberg need water? *No.*

Does an iceberg need air? *No*.
Does an iceberg grow? *No*.

An iceberg is not a living thing.

Penguin

Is a penguin a living thing?

ice – frozen water

Does a penguin need food? *Yes.*
Does a penguin need water? *Yes.*

Does a penguin need air? *Yes.*

Does a penguin grow? *Yes.*

So a penguin is a living thing.

A polar region is home to many things. A polar region is an

important habitat.

Picture glossary

habitat area where plants and animals live

iceberg large piece of floating ice

polar region a habitat that is very cold

Index

habitat   4, 22–23

iceberg   14–17, 23

penguin   18–21

polar bear   6–9

whale   10–13

Notes for parents and teachers
Before reading
Talk to the children about living and non-living things. Ask them how they would know
if something is living or non-living. Help them to come to some conclusions about the
characteristics of both living and non-living things.
After reading
Show children where the polar regions are on a globe. Talk about icebergs which float
in the Artic and Antarctic oceans. Fill a small bag full of water and freeze it. Then place
the ice lump in a tray of water. Talk about floating and how there is more of the iceberg
below the water than above.
Look at the DVD or read the book *March of the Penguins*. Talk about the environment
where the penguins live.